KIJC

P9-APJ-624

OUR GREAT STATES

WHAT'S GREAT ABOUT
CALIFORNIA?

* Anita Yasuda

🝰 LERNER PUBLICATIONS COMPANY * MINNEAPOLIS

CONTENTS

THIS IS CALIFORNIA! ✴ 4

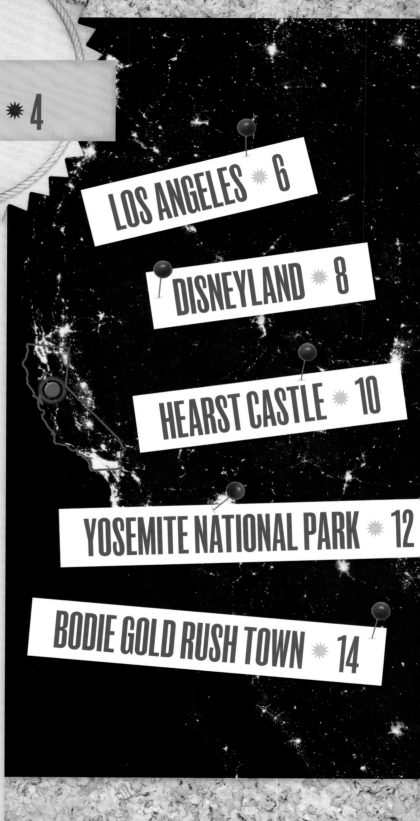

Content Consultant: Zevi Gutfreund, Assistant Professor of History, Louisiana State University

Lerner Publications Company
A division of Lerner Publishing Group, Inc.
241 First Avenue North
Minneapolis, MN 55401 USA

For reading levels and more information, look up this title at www.lernerbooks.com.

Main body text set in ITC Franklin Gothic Std Book Condensed 12/15.
Typeface provided by Adobe Systems.

Library of Congress Cataloging-in-Publication Data

Yasuda, Anita.
    What's great about California? / by Anita Yasuda.
        pages   cm. — (Our great states)
    Includes index.
    ISBN 978–1–4677–3349–6 (lib. bdg. : alk. paper)
    ISBN 978–1–4677–4706–6 (eBook)
    1. California—Juvenile literature. I. Title.
F861.3.Y37 2015
979.4—dc23   201304511

Manufactured in the United States of America
1 – PC – 7/15/14

This Is CALIFORNIA!

California has endless sunshine, warm days, and miles of coastline. Each spring, fields sparkle with yellow poppies. No wonder California's nickname is the Golden State. California has miles of sandy beaches along the Pacific Ocean. Santa Cruz Beach Boardwalk is one of the oldest seaside amusement parks in the United States. Can you hear the screams from the spinning roller coaster or the music from the antique carousel? California is known for having tons of fun outdoor activities. Surf on the ocean. Or head for the mountains and strap on a snowboard. California is also famous for movie stars and film studios. The state has a lot to see and do. Read on to learn about ten great places to visit in California.

OREGON

KLAMATH MOUNTAINS

Klamath River

CASCADE MOUNTAINS

Sacramento River

GREAT BASIN DESERT

NEVADA

Lake Tahoe

● Sacramento

San Francisco ● Oakland

San Francisco Bay

● San Jose

San Joaquin River

S I E R R A   N E V A D A

Yosemite National Park

● Monterey

● Fresno

GREAT BASIN DESERT

▲ Mount Whitney

Bakersfield ●

Death Valley National Park

Los Angeles ●

MOJAVE DESERT

● Anaheim

Channel Islands

Long Beach

COLORADO DESERT

San Diego ●

U.S.A.
MEXICO

ARIZONA

N

Miles
0   50   100

0   50   100   150
Kilometers

PACIFIC OCEAN

Explore California's beaches and all the places in between. Just turn the page to find out all about the GOLDEN STATE. >

59763

LOS ANGELES

THE ACADEMY AWARDS

In the early 1900s, California's frequent sunny days attracted film studios. The film industry created many jobs. In 1929, one of the biggest events in entertainment began. It is now known as the Academy Awards. These awards celebrate everything about the movies.

> Saber-toothed cats once lived in what is now Los Angeles. They left their footprints behind in the middle of the city. Go on a flashlight tour of the La Brea Tar Pits. La Brea is a forty-thousand-year-old oil field. It is now part of the Page Museum. It has fossils of more than one million animals that became trapped in the goo.

But don't stop there! Los Angeles has a lot more to discover. Hop on a tour bus. Snap photos of the Hollywood sign. Listen to musicians on lively Olvera Street, the oldest area in Los Angeles. Or look for your favorite star's name on the Hollywood Walk of Fame in front of TCL Chinese Theatre. The Hollywood Walk of Fame honors people in entertainment. It has more than two thousand stars. Each star has a celebrity's name on it. Some stars even have celebrities' footprints or handprints.

At the Santa Monica Pier, ride the world's only solar-powered Ferris wheel. From here, head over to Venice Beach. Check out the street performers. Who knows? Maybe you'll be part of the show!

See for yourself the footprints of animals trapped in the La Brea Tar Pits over the centuries.

The Hollywood Walk of Fame is more than 3.5 miles (5.6 kilometers) long.

DISNEYLAND

> Spinning teacups, flying elephants, and a roller coaster zooming through a mountain. These are just some of the attractions at Disneyland in Anaheim. It is the most popular amusement park in the world.

Walt Disney was an animator and screenwriter. One of his most famous characters is Mickey Mouse. The first Mickey Mouse cartoon came out in 1928. People loved Mickey! On July 17, 1955, Walt Disney opened his theme park. He built the park on 160 acres (64 hectares) of former orange groves.

Fourteen million people visit Disneyland each year. Watch a parade. Meet some of the famous Disney characters. Enjoy a jungle cruise or take a ride with Peter Pan in a flying pirate ship. And don't miss the fireworks above Sleeping Beauty's Castle. They happen almost every night. Special guest Tinker Bell always makes a visit. So put on your mouse ears and find out why Disneyland is magical.

If you're an *Alice in Wonderland* fan, you'll love the Mad Tea Party ride.

Bronze statues of Walt Disney and Mickey Mouse greet visitors in front of Cinderella Castle.

HEARST CASTLE

> Presidents and movie stars have stayed at the Hearst Castle overlooking the Pacific Ocean. It is so close to the ocean that you can hear the sound of the crashing waves. The castle is near the town of San Simeon. That is halfway between Los Angeles and San Francisco.

The castle's former owner, William Randolph Hearst, owned twenty-six newspapers. He wanted to build a castle in the hills of California. It took nearly thirty years to build. The castle was never completely finished. Hearst had to stop living there in 1947 because of health problems.

As you board the bus to the castle, be on the lookout for cattle. They graze on grassland that is part of Hearst Ranch below the castle. Once you arrive at the castle, you will see some of the 165 rooms. Hearst filled the rooms with statues and paintings. See if you can find all 61 bathrooms. There is a movie theater and a huge pool. During the 1920s and the 1930s, the castle also had an airstrip. Don't leave without seeing the zoo. It was once the largest private zoo in the world.

The pool at the Hearst Castle is surrounded by Roman columns.

Look for the zebras on the grounds of the Hearst Castle as you drive in from San Simeon.

YOSEMITE NATIONAL PARK

Yosemite Falls is actually made up of three separate falls.

> A forested road leads to huge granite mountains. This is Yosemite National Park. Look up! You might see hikers climbing the famous Half Dome. This 8,839-foot (2,694-meter) granite dome looks like it has been cut in half. The only way to reach the top is on metal cables.

Yosemite is 180 miles (289 km) southeast of Sacramento. The park is known for its natural wonders. Check out the groves of giant sequoia trees. Some are more than 250 feet (76 m) tall! The fourth-highest waterfall in North America is also found here. Yosemite Falls is 2,425 feet (739 m) tall.

Yosemite is one of the most popular parks in the United States. Close to four million people visit each year. You could be one of them! Take photographs. Climb the rocks. Hike along one of the park's trails. It has 800 miles (1,287 km) of them. Mule or horse rides offer a one-of-a-kind adventure through the park.

Don't miss the chance to saddle up at Yosemite!

BODIE GOLD RUSH TOWN

Peek inside the windows of the original buildings still standing in Bodie.

> Imagine horses and antique wagons driving down a dusty road. Step back in time to explore an abandoned mining town. It is California's official gold rush ghost town, Bodie.

Bodie was named after W. S. Bodey. In 1859, he found gold east of the Sierra Nevada. Like many gold rush towns, Bodie sprung up almost overnight. It was a busy town. At its peak, Bodie had nearly ten thousand people. But when the gold and silver had been mined, the people left.

Bodie is a ghost town. No one lives there. It is part of the California State Parks System. About one hundred buildings stand along its dusty street. Listen to a history talk or go on a tour of the old Bodie mill. Read all about the gold rush at the bookstore in the museum. Explore the original general store. What secrets will you find behind the doors? Maybe you will even see a ghost!

FORTY-NINERS

In 1848, James Marshall was building a sawmill on the American River for wealthy businessman John Sutter. One day, Marshall noticed something in the river. It was gold! A year after his discovery, thousands of people came to California. They came to be known as Forty-Niners. This was because they left for the gold fields in the year 1849.

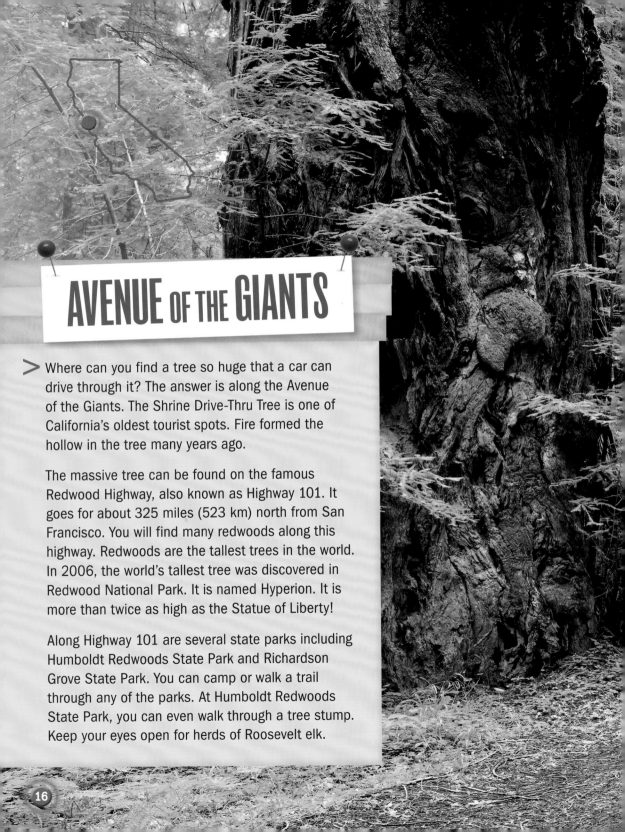

AVENUE OF THE GIANTS

> Where can you find a tree so huge that a car can drive through it? The answer is along the Avenue of the Giants. The Shrine Drive-Thru Tree is one of California's oldest tourist spots. Fire formed the hollow in the tree many years ago.

The massive tree can be found on the famous Redwood Highway, also known as Highway 101. It goes for about 325 miles (523 km) north from San Francisco. You will find many redwoods along this highway. Redwoods are the tallest trees in the world. In 2006, the world's tallest tree was discovered in Redwood National Park. It is named Hyperion. It is more than twice as high as the Statue of Liberty!

Along Highway 101 are several state parks including Humboldt Redwoods State Park and Richardson Grove State Park. You can camp or walk a trail through any of the parks. At Humboldt Redwoods State Park, you can even walk through a tree stump. Keep your eyes open for herds of Roosevelt elk.

Drive through a redwood on northern California's Redwood Highway.

TOUR THRU TREE

At Humboldt Redwoods State Park, you can go inside tree houses made from redwood trunks.

BALBOA PARK

> Puppet shows, movie nights, and wild animals make San Diego's Balboa Park one of the most exciting parks in California. It is 1,200 acres (485 ha) of fun! One of the best ways to see the park is by train. The miniature train might be small, but it has its own conductor and specially designed tracks.

Hop off the train and see the world-famous San Diego Zoo. This zoo within the park is home to more than four thousand amazing animals. You'll have lots of chances to make new wildlife friends. Have your picture taken with a cheetah. You can even touch and feed a rhino! Maybe you can spot koalas hiding in a tree. Or go on an overnight safari and sleep at the zoo. Who knows what you will see?

Before leaving the park, take a ride on the 1910 Carousel. It's more than one hundred years old! You might want to spend a few more days at Balboa Park. There are fifteen museums to see. You would not want to miss a ride in a spaceship at the San Diego Air and Space Museum!

The giant pandas at the San Diego Zoo are big attractions.

EL CAMINO REAL

Beginning in the year 1769, Spanish monks built twenty-one missions along the California coast. They wanted to teach American Indians about Christianity. The road between the missions was called El Camino Real. It means "Royal Highway." By horseback, it took the monks one day to travel from one mission to the next. El Camino Real stretches between San Diego in the south to San Francisco in the north.

GOLDEN GATE BRIDGE

> A bright orange bridge slices across the San Francisco skyline. It is the Golden Gate Bridge. The Golden Gate Bridge is a San Francisco landmark. It is the twelfth-longest suspension bridge in the world. A suspension bridge is a bridge that is hung from two or more cables held up by towers. The bridge is 0.8 miles (1.3 km) long.

The Golden Gate Bridge stretches between the city of San Francisco and Marin County. It was built over a narrow strip of water called the Golden Gate. Two hundred thousand people walked across the bridge on opening day, May 27, 1937.

If you go to the bridge, rent a bike to see the wonderful views of the Pacific Ocean and San Francisco Bay. Visit the Bridge Round House, which overlooks the bridge. Go on a guided bridge tour. See the breathtaking photos at the Bridge Photo Experience. Listen to the stories of how this amazing bridge was built at the Bridge Pavilion. After your bridge walk, you can take a hike on the Coastal and Bay Trails nearby.

More than one hundred thousand cars cross the Golden Gate Bridge each day.

GOLDEN GATE BRIDGE
MAIN SPAN
4200 FEET

LENGTH OF ONE CABLE .... 7650 FT / 2332m
DIAMETER OF ONE CABLE .... 36 1/8 IN / 92.4 cm
WIRES IN EACH CABLE 27,572
TOTAL WIRE USED .... 80,000 MILES / 128,748 km
WEIGHT OF CABLE .... 24,500 TONS / 22,226 m tons

Cable Constructor: John A. Roebling's Sons Co.
Trenton & Roebling, New Jersey

BRIDGE CONSTRUCTION

Work began on the Golden Gate Bridge on January 5, 1933. It was a difficult job. Workers faced high winds and rough waters. Eleven men lost their lives during the construction. It took four years to build. The bridge has always been painted International Orange. The architects chose the orange color to make the bridge easier for passing ships to see.

DEATH VALLEY

> You can't miss a national park in California that's almost double the size of the state of Delaware. It is called Death Valley National Park. Death Valley is the lowest place in North America. Its elevation is 282 feet (86 m) below sea level. It is also the hottest place in the world. A record temperature was set in 1913. Temperatures reached 134°F (57°C)!

More than eight hundred thousand people per year come to see Death Valley. Maybe you will be one of them. Put on your boots and hike up to Natural Bridge Canyon. Rabbits and lizards will share the trails with you. Be on the lookout for mountain lions!

Don't miss the highest sand dunes in all of California. The Eureka Dunes are 3 miles (4.8 km) long and 1 mile (1.6 km) wide. While climbing the dunes, you might hear the sand sing! When the grains of sand move underfoot, they make sounds as loud as an airplane. These booming sounds are made when very dry sand slides over itself.

You might see a bighorn sheep in Death Valley National Park.

The rock bridge spanning the gap at Natural Bridge Canyon is 50 feet (15 m) high.

23

The average cell in Alcatraz was 5 feet (1.5 m) by 9 feet (2.7 m).

ALCATRAZ

> Sitting in the middle of San Francisco Bay is a rocky island. On it is a famous former prison called Alcatraz. It was known as the Rock. When it was in use, it was the toughest prison to escape from in the United States. Alcatraz opened as a federal prison in 1934. Some of the United States' worst criminals were sent here. Chicago crime boss Al Capone and bank robber George "Machine Gun Kelly" Barnes had cells in Alcatraz.

Alcatraz was made into a national park after it was no longer used as a prison. Thousands of people visit each day. If you go to Alcatraz, the ferry ride over is super fun. You will have great views of the Golden Gate Bridge and other attractions such as Coit Tower.

Once you're on the island, be ready to climb! The road zigs and zags up to the prison. Inside, walk through the cell blocks. Listen to stories about people who tried to escape but could not. Some say that ghosts haunt the prison! You never know whom you will see at Alcatraz.

Coit Tower, *(above right)*, is a 210-foot-high (64 m) San Francisco landmark.

YOUR TOP TEN

Now that you have read about ten awesome things to see and do in California, think about what your California top ten list would include. If you were planning a California vacation, what would you like to see? Make your top ten list on a separate sheet of paper. If you would like, you can turn your list into a booklet. You can add drawings or pictures from the Internet or magazines.

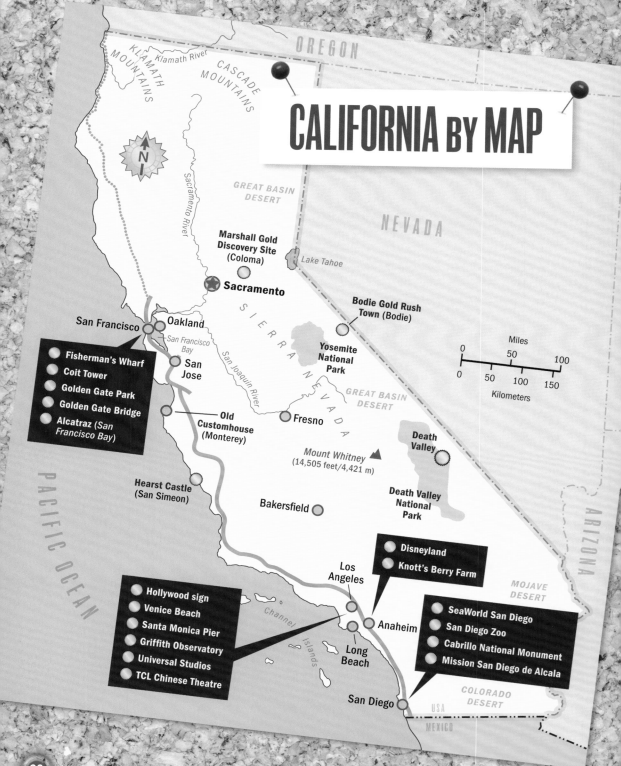

CALIFORNIA BY MAP

OREGON

KLAMATH MOUNTAINS

Klamath River

CASCADE MOUNTAINS

GREAT BASIN DESERT

NEVADA

Marshall Gold Discovery Site (Coloma)

Lake Tahoe

Sacramento River

★ **Sacramento**

Bodie Gold Rush Town (Bodie)

San Francisco

Oakland

San Francisco Bay

San Jose

San Joaquin River

SIERRA NEVADA

Yosemite National Park

GREAT BASIN DESERT

Miles
0   50   100
0   50   100   150
Kilometers

- Fisherman's Wharf
- Coit Tower
- Golden Gate Park
- Golden Gate Bridge
- Alcatraz (San Francisco Bay)

Old Customhouse (Monterey)

Fresno

Mount Whitney (14,505 feet/4,421 m)

Death Valley

Hearst Castle (San Simeon)

Bakersfield

Death Valley National Park

ARIZONA

Los Angeles

- Disneyland
- Knott's Berry Farm

MOJAVE DESERT

PACIFIC OCEAN

- Hollywood sign
- Venice Beach
- Santa Monica Pier
- Griffith Observatory
- Universal Studios
- TCL Chinese Theatre

Channel Islands

Anaheim

Long Beach

- SeaWorld San Diego
- San Diego Zoo
- Cabrillo National Monument
- Mission San Diego de Alcala

San Diego

USA

MEXICO

COLORADO DESERT

> MAP KEY

⊛ Capital city

◯ City

◯ Point of interest

▲ Highest elevation

···— International border

—·— State border

— El Camino Real

······ Redwood Highway/
Avenue of the Giants

Visit www.lerneresource.com
to learn more about the state
flag of California.

CALIFORNIA REPUBLIC

CALIFORNIA FACTS

NICKNAME: The Golden State

SONG: "I Love You, California" by F. B. Silverwood and A. F. Frankenstein

MOTTO: "Eureka"

FLOWER: poppy

TREE: redwood

BIRD: quail

ANIMAL: grizzly bear

FOODS: avocado, artichoke,

DATE AND RANK OF STATEHOOD: September 9, 1850; the 31st state

CAPITAL: Sacramento

AREA: 155,779 square miles (403,467 sq. km)

AVERAGE JANUARY TEMPERATURE: 63°F (17°C)

AVERAGE JULY TEMPERATURE: 75°F (24°C)

POPULATION AND RANK: 38,041,430; 1st (2012)

MAJOR CITIES AND POPULATIONS: Los Angeles (3,863,839), San Diego (1,326,238), San Jose (984,299)

NUMBER OF US CONGRESS MEMBERS: 53 representatives; 2 senators

NUMBER OF ELECTORAL VOTES: 55

NATURAL RESOURCES: water, seafood, fish, forests, minerals, diatomite, gold, gypsum, potash, pumice, sand and gravel, tungsten, natural gas and oil

AGRICULTURAL PRODUCTS: milk, grapes, oranges, almonds, cattle, strawberries, lettuce, walnuts, hay, tomatoes

MANUFACTURED GOODS: computers, electronics, aircraft, cars, telecommunications equipment, wine

HOLIDAYS AND CELEBRATIONS: Tournament of Roses, Pasadena; Chinese New Year Celebration, San Francisco and Los Angeles; Cherry Blossom Festival, San Francisco

GLOSSARY

animator: an artist who draws cartoons

antique: very old or from a long time ago

cattle: cows, bulls, or steers that are kept on a farm

conductor: a person in charge of a train

dune: a hill made from sand

elevation: the height above sea level

general store: a store that sells many things such as food and clothing

granite: a hard rock

mission: a church or place where people sent to a foreign country to teach about religion live and work

mule: an animal that is part donkey and part horse

safari: a trip taken to see large wild animals

sawmill: a building where logs are made into boards

screenwriter: a person who writes stories for films

sea level: the average level of the ocean's surface

solar-powered: to run on energy from the sun

LERNER

SOURCE

Expand learning beyond the printed book. Download free, complementary educational resources for this book from our website, www.lerneresource.com.

FURTHER INFORMATION

Duffield, Katy S. *California History for Kids: Mission, Miners, and Moviemakers in the Golden State*. Chicago: Chicago Review Press, 2012. This activity-packed book introduces readers to the rich history of California.

Friedman, Mel. *The California Gold Rush*. New York: Scholastic Children's Press, 2010. Read the true story of people from all around the world coming to California in search of gold.

The Library of Congress—America's Story
http://www.americaslibrary.gov
Explore this site to learn about amazing Americans from the past and to explore each state.

Nelson, Libby, and Kari Cornell. *California Missions Projects and Layouts*. Minneapolis: Lerner Publications, 2008. Build models of California's twenty-one missions by following the detailed instructions. Information and illustrations of each mission's history are included.

Oakland Museum of California
http://www.museumca.org/goldrush
Visit this site to take a virtual tour of the Oakland Museum of California's gold rush exhibition.

State of California—Kids Portal
http://www.ca.gov/HomeFamily/ChildrenFamilies/JustForKids
Visit this site from the State of California to learn more about California governors, missions, and history.

INDEX

PHOTO ACKNOWLEDGMENTS

The images in this book are used with the permission of: © holbox/Shutterstock Images, p. 1; © Paul Topp /Dreamstime.com, p. 4; © alacatr/iStockphoto, pp. 4–5; © Lerner Publications, pp. 5, 26–27; © Helen King/Corbis, pp. 6–7; © Joe Seer /Shutterstock Images, p. 6; © Bambi L. Dingman /Dreamstime.com, p. 7 (top); © Jabiru/Dreamstime .com, p. 7 (bottom); © Christian Ender/dpa/Corbis, pp. 8–9; © Starletdarlene/Dreamstime.com, p. 8; © Pfong001/Dreamstime.com, p. 9; © Craig Aurness/Hearst Castle/CA Park Service/Corbis, pp. 10–11; © Vlad G/Shutterstock Images, p. 11 (top); © George D. Lepp/Hearst Castle/CA Park Service/CORBIS, p. 11 (bottom); © Ringo Chiu/ ZUMA Press/Corbis, pp. 12–1 ; © Nathan Jaskowiak /Shutterstock Images, p. 12; © John Turner /Dreamstime.com, p. 13; © Gavin Hellier/Robert Harding World Imagery/Corbis, pp. 14–15; © Hanze /Shutterstock Images, p. 14; © duncan1890 /iStockphoto, p. 15; © Douglas Orton/Spaces Images/Corbis, pp. 16–17; © Cheryle Myers /Dreamstime.com, p. 17 (top); © Caro/Alamy, p. 17 (bottom); © Andrew Zarivny/Shutterstock Images, pp. 18–19, 29 (bottom); © Richard Cummins/Design Pics/Corbis, 19 (top); © Nadia Borisevich /Shutterstock Images, 19 (bottom); © RX2 Photography/Shutterstock Images, pp. 20–21; © Neil Lang/Shutterstock Images, p. 21 (top); © Martin D. Vonka/Shutterstock Images, p. 21 (bottom); © Escudero Patrick/Hemis/Corbis, pp. 22–23; © Nickolay Stanev/Shutterstock Images, p. 23 (top); © Angel DiBilio/Shutterstock Images, 23 (bottom); © Sergio Pitamitz/Corbis, pp. 24–25; © Luke James Ritchie/Shutterstock Images, p. 24; © Click Images/Shutterstock Images, p. 25; © Globe Turner/Shutterstock Images, p. 29 (top); © Malgorzata Litkowska/Shutterstock Images, p. 29 (middle, top); © Ian Maton/Shutterstock, p. 29 (middle, bottom); © Joanne Harris and Daniel Bubnich/Shutterstock Images, p. 29 (bottom).

Cover: © Dan Breckwoldt/Shutterstock.com (Hollywood) © ventusdud/Shutterstock.com (Golden Gate Bridge); © Mikhail Klesnikov/Shutterstock.com (Yosemite). © Mariusz S. Jurgielewicz /Shutterstock.com (Bodie, CA); © Laura Westlund/ Independent Picture Service (map); © iStockphoto. com/fpm (seal); © iStockphoto.com/vicm (pushpins); © iStockphoto.com/benz190 (corkboard).